Police Officers

By Rachel Tisdale

CRABTREE
Publishing Company
www.crabtreebooks.com

The World's MOST DANGEROUS Jobs

Author: Rachel Tisdale
Managing editor: Paul Humphrey
Editorial director: Kathy Middleton
Editor: Adrianna Morganelli
Proofreader: Rachel Eagen
Series Design: Elaine Wilkinson
Page Design: sprout.uk.com
Cover design: Margaret Salter
Production coordinator: Margaret Salter
Prepress technician: Margaret Salter
Print coordinator: Katherine Berti

Photo credits:
DEA: page 18 (inset)
Getty Images: pages 16 (Dan Kitwood), 17 (Stringer/AFP), 20–21 (Johan Ordonez/AFP), 22–23 (Marco Georgiev), 27 (Dan Istitene), 29 (bottom) (Massoud Hossaini/AFP)
Photoshot: pages 1 (Grzegorz Michalowski), 6 (Jim and Mary Whitmer), 18 (left) (Weng Xinyang)
Shutterstock: pages 5 (Katarzyna Mazurowska), 9 (Tumar), 10–11 (Greg Goodman), 12 (grafvision), 24 (Ron Kacmarcik), 29 (top) (Duard van der Westhuizen), cover (top)
Thinkstock: Comstock: cover (bottom)
VisionMetric Ltd: page 13, West Midlands Police: pages 14–15, 25

COVER STORY

◄ **COVER (top) – Police guard a bank during a riot in London, England.**

◄ **COVER (bottom) – A police officer uses a special computer mounted in his car.**

PAGE 1 – Mounted police officers patrol a street in Lodz, Poland.

Library and Archives Canada Cataloguing in Publication

Tisdale, Rachel
    Police officers / Rachel Tisdale.

(The world's most dangerous jobs)
Includes index.
Issued also in electronic format.
ISBN 978-0-7787-5101-4 (bound).--ISBN 978-0-7787-5115-1 (pbk.)

    1. Police--Juvenile literature. I. Title.
II. Series: World's most dangerous jobs

HV7922.T57 2012   j363.2'3   C2012-901571-7

Library of Congress Cataloging-in-Publication Data

Tisdale, Rachel.
    Police officers / Rachel Tisdale.
        p. cm. -- (The world's most dangerous jobs)
    Includes index.
    ISBN 978-0-7787-5101-4 (reinforced library binding : alk. paper) --
ISBN 978-0-7787-5115-1 (pbk. : alk. paper) -- ISBN 978-1-4271-8071-1
(electronic pdf) -- ISBN 978-1-4271-8075-9 (electronic html)
    1. Police--Juvenile literature. I. Title.

HV7922.T57 2012
363.2--dc23

2012008523

Crabtree Publishing Company
www.crabtreebooks.com   1-800-387-7650

Printed in Canada/042012/KR20120316

Published in Canada
Crabtree Publishing
616 Welland Ave.
St. Catharines, Ontario
L2M 5V6

Published in the United States
Crabtree Publishing
PMB 59051
350 Fifth Avenue, 59th Floor
New York, New York 10118

Published in the United Kingdom
Crabtree Publishing
Maritime House
Basin Road North, Hove
BN41 1WR

Published in Australia
Crabtree Publishing
3 Charles Street
Coburg North
VIC 3058

CONTENTS

Glossary words defined on p. 31 are in **bold** the first time they appear in the text.

POLICE OFFICERS

Most people go to work knowing that nothing dangerous will happen to them and they will go home safe to their families at the end of the day. However, some jobs involve facing danger on a regular basis. Being a police officer can be one of the world's most dangerous jobs.

Police officers arrive at work not knowing what their shift might involve. They may pursue a stolen car at dangerously high speeds, come face to face with armed criminals, or carry out a raid on a gang hideout. These are just some of the dangers that a police officer may face.

Police officers are a vital part of keeping any country safe. They are trained to handle dangerous situations and to protect the public. Yet thousands of police officers are assaulted and injured every year. Hundreds are killed in the line of duty. They make the ultimate sacrifice just by doing their jobs.

> "I am outstandingly proud of our officers who put themselves in positions of danger on a daily basis."
>
> Tony Eastaugh, Commander of London's Metropolitan Police, UK

► A special weapons and tactics team (S.W.A.T.) descends a building to investigate a dangerous situation inside.

PROTECTING AGAINST DANGER

▼ These police officers wear some of the standard equipment issued amongst the force.

"A more brazen, cold-blooded criminal element is on the prowl in America, and they don't think twice about killing a cop."

Craig W. Floyd,
Chairman of the National Law Enforcement Officers Memorial Fund

Police officers are issued with special equipment to help keep them safe. This equipment varies for each police force around the world.

Here is just some of the equipment that officers use:

Firearms and bullets: In most countries, officers carry firearms. Standard equipment is a small handgun and ammunition. In a few countries, including the United Kingdom, New Zealand, Norway, and Iceland, only specially trained firearms officers carry weapons.

Body armor: Many police forces issue body armor to their police officers.

Baton: Police officers use a telescopic baton, which expands and collapses easily and quickly.

Flashlight: Police officers frequently work at night.

Chemical spray: Officers carry a chemical spray, and, if faced with danger, they spray it into an aggressor's face.

Handcuffs: Police officers often need to restrain dangerous suspects.

Personal protection pouch (PPP): The PPP contains gloves, in case an officer needs to handle anything dangerous, and a **cardiopulmonary resuscitation (CPR)** mask.

Taser: Some police officers now carry **Tasers**. Police officers can use this weapon by shooting it or pressing it against someone. It gives out an electric shock that makes the recipient unable to move for a short time.

TRAINING POLICE OFFICERS

Police officers deal with a wide range of situations, from arresting criminals and carrying out emergency first aid, to helping victims of crime. Once candidates have been successfully selected for a force they start their basic training to become police officers.

Basic training teaches officers the laws they must uphold and the correct procedures for dealing with suspects. They learn about officer safety and first aid, and they have to improve their physical fitness. There is an emphasis on communication and health and safety, as well as human rights.

Police officers then go on to serve a two-year probation period under the guidance of a training officer. During this time police officers attend real calls and deal with them while being assessed.

At the end of probationary training, qualified police officers go out on patrol on foot, bicycle, in a patrol vehicle, **mounted unit**, or motorcycle. They may choose to specialize in a certain area, like the traffic police, dog handling, **air support units**, underwater units, counter terrorism, and many more.

"Basic training teaches you all the skills you need to be a police officer, but there is nothing like the hands-on experience of doing the job. On my first day of probationary training I had to change a light bulb for an elderly person who was sitting in the dark! Then I was called to a house fire where a whole family tragically died."

PC Sharon Campbell, Strathclyde police, Scotland

USING FIREARMS

Every time police officers knock on a suspect's door or pull over a car on the highway, they never know what will happen. There could be an armed terrorists in the house, or a dangerous criminal behind the wheel. To deal with this, police officers in most countries are issued firearms and trained to use them properly.

Armed police officers are trained to react quickly and efficiently, but without sacrificing safety. During training, officers are confronted with realistic scenarios designed to reflect actual deadly-force incidents that they may encounter when performing their jobs.

"It takes a certain type of person to deal with [S.W.A.T.] situations...You want a certain maturity level, someone who is not easily flustered."

Captain Randy Pennington, Huntersville, NC, Police Department

When the police know they are facing a very dangerous situation, such as entering a drug gang's hideout, they employ a S.W.A.T. team. These teams are issued more substantial firearms such as sub-machine guns, sniper rifles, **suppressed weapons** and chemical agents. Their job is to protect civilians and police personnel while reducing the possibility of death in high-risk incidents.

▶ Although issued with firearms, police officers undergo thorough training to help them safely deal with violent criminals without the need to use guns.

11

EMERGENCY!

▲ An E-FIT sketch

A call goes out:
"Any officers in the area ...an armed robbery is taking place..."

Police officers race to the scene, lights flashing and siren screaming. Dog handlers and other specialist units are called in. At the scene two suspects are aiming weapons at a cashier and other citizens are being held hostage in the store. What do you do? How do you react?

Police officers may have to deal with an emergency like this every week, but they are trained to cope in such stressful situations. Officers stay calm, which reduces the risk of the offender becoming agitated. It also helps the officers to clearly observe the situation and ensure their own safety. A specialist **police negotiator** may be needed to talk to offenders and try to resolve the situation as quickly as possible. If things get dangerous, tactical units are used to enter the building and face offenders.

The offenders may have escaped before the police arrive. It is the job of the officers on the scene to gather evidence from witnesses and **closed-circuit TV (CCTV)**. Police can put together an **E-FIT** (Electronic Facial Identification Technique) sketch from witness descriptions and issue an arrest warrant throughout the force in an attempt to catch them. A huge team of police officers are involved in such an emergency, many of whom put their own lives at risk.

"(Guns are) a fashion accessory now."

Chief Constable Paul Acres

TRAFFIC POLICE

A traffic police officer faces many dangers on the streets every day. Pursuing stolen vehicles at very high speeds, safely apprehending drunk drivers, and performing regular vehicle stops are just some of the many jobs that traffic officers undertake. Officers have to undergo rigorous training to prove their driving ability before they are assigned to the traffic police.

▲ In the United Kingdom, the word "POLICE" is written backward so that motorists can read it in their driving mirrors.

Some traffic officers drive unmarked vehicles, so law-breakers can't detect them. These vehicles usually have very powerful engines. Traffic officers must be vigilant and responsive during a car chase. They have to make split-second decisions as to whether it is safe, to the public and the traffic officers themselves, to continue, especially on crowded city streets or a busy highway.

A traffic officer may sometimes need a helping hand from an air support unit. Specialist helicopter units provide an "eye in the sky" view for the traffic police on the ground. The helicopters are fitted with heat-seeking cameras to detect criminals if they run from their vehicles. These helicopter units face many dangers, especially while flying at night in city areas where there are radio masts, tall buildings and high-voltage power lines to be avoided.

▲ Traffic police officers sometimes travel at dangerous speeds in order to catch fleeing criminals.

> "Dealing with the aftermath of a serious or fatal collision is never pleasant, but it makes me even more determined to prevent as many injuries and deaths on the roads as I can."
>
> Andrew Tate, traffic officer

TERRORIST THREATS

After the catastrophic terrorist attacks on the World Trade Center in New York and the London and Mumbai bombings, governments realized that terrorism is very much an everyday threat in today's society. Police officers around the world are trying to prevent such attacks happening in the future. They are also tackling, observing, disrupting, and bringing those responsible for such attacks to justice, in an effort to keep our countries safe.

◄ Airport security procedures throughout the world heightened after the September 11 attacks. Airport police are now often armed, even in those countries where officers do not usually carry firearms.

A police officer may be faced with a group of armed terrorists with a plane full of hostages, the release of a biological weapon, or a suicide bomber strapped with explosives, all of which are highly dangerous, life-threatening situations. To deal with such terrorist threats quickly and effectively some police officers undergo counter-terrorism training to learn the skills needed to deal with these emergencies.

Dedicated counter-terrorism police units are set up all over the world to carry out secret investigations and intelligence gathering. This undercover police observation of extremist groups is a key element in the prevention of terrorist attacks. Officers may listen in and observe a group's movements for months and even years, gathering evidence to bring such groups and their members to justice before they commit their crimes.

"The global threat of extremism and terrorism has to be met by all... taking a very tough and hard line..."

Former U.S. Secretary of State Condoleezza Rice

▶ S.W.A.T. police officers storm a bus during a counter-terrorism training exercise.

17

◄ Police officers target drug traffickers in a raid in Rio de Janeiro, Brazil.

▼ Police officers recover millions of dollars worth of illegal substances every year. Weapons are also a real threat to officers tackling this undercover world.

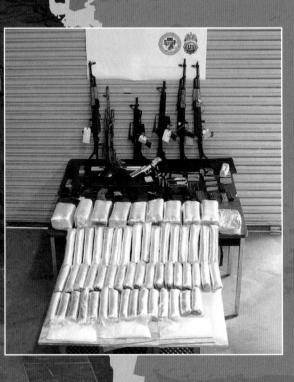

DRUGS

Police officers tackle the war on the illegal drugs trade on many levels, from apprehending a small drugs dealer handing over packets on street corners, bringing down major **drug cartels**. This war against the illegal drugs trade is a highly dangerous one, where hundreds of people, including police officers, are murdered every year.

One of the most dangerous jobs for officers is to go undercover. They have to **infiltrate** and become one with those involved in the criminal world of drugs. Undercover officers have to be very secretive and face real risks if they are suspected. These officers can lead a secret life for several years, gathering evidence to bring criminals to justice.

> The gangster pulled his car over on a dark country lane. He stuck the barrel of his gun into my mouth: 'You're a cozzer (police officer), aren't you?' Any hint of doubt in his mind and I would have been killed; my body dumped. Training had prepared me for this moment. I didn't flinch....
>
> **Liam Thomas, ex-undercover police officer**

Specially trained dog units are used to sniff out drugs in airports, vehicles or on people. The dogs live with their officers and undergo extensive training where they are taught to detect drugs. Drugs dogs can even detect money that has been in contact with drugs at some point.

GANGS

Gang violence around the world is one of the most extreme dangers facing police officers. Some countries have specialist police units to combat the problem of gangs. Gangs commit crimes such as robbery, assaults, murder, and kidnapping, and can be involved in drug and **people trafficking** and prostitution.

► Armed gang members stand guard at the entrance to their street territory.

"If you do something to them, their natural response is, 'OK, I'm going to kill you'...Or at least they talk like they will."

A spokesman from Prince George's County's Police, Sgt. George Norris

Police officers themselves can often be targets following crackdowns on gangs and gang-related crime. It can be a slow and painful process trying to bring gang members to justice, when every day officers are being shot, stabbed, and sometimes violently murdered by gang members.

One of the world's most notorious gangs, Mara Salvatrucha, also known as MS-13, has over 10,000 members in the U.S. who are known for their exceedingly violent methods. While most of this gang's violence is directed toward rival street gangs and its own members, innocent citizens and police officers have also fallen victim to this gang.

> Gangs have changed with the times, and have gotten more sophisticated, and have used technology to assist in their crimes. They have also gotten more violent toward police... Too many good cops have been killed by gang members.

Timothy Brennan, former Peace Officer for the Compton Police Department, California

DISASTER AREAS

When an area is hit by the devastating effects of a natural disaster, it is up to the police to make the area safe and secure for the public. Police officers patrol bridges where the waters below rage violently, they evacuate stranded residents and pets from their flooded homes, and help with the rescue efforts after buildings have collapsed in earthquakes.

Police officers risk losing their lives in such dangerous situations. In Cumbria, England, in 2009, police officer Bill Barker was directing motorists to safety after torrential rain had caused rivers to flood, when he was swept away in the floodwaters.

▼ Police officers rescue a stranded woman from her flooded home in New Orleans, during the aftermath of Hurricane Katrina.

Hurricane Katrina, New Orleans

In August 2005, hurricane Katrina battered the Florida coastline and the storm passed directly through New Orleans, with winds blasting at 124 mph (200 km/h) leaving hundreds of homes destroyed and thousands of residents homeless. The Louisiana Superdome was used as an evacuation center, where around 20,000 people sought refuge. The shortage of supplies soon led to unrest, tension, and lootings. It was down to police officers to make the area safe.

"One police officer has already been shot by looters. There are rescue workers risking their lives to save people trapped in their homes, and now these heroes and the survivors are in danger from armed looters."

Jessica Marrero, New Orleans, LA, 2005

WATER POLICE

The water, or marine police fight crime, prevent disorder, and help to keep our waterways safe. A typical day at work might involve chasing drug smugglers, searching for a murder victim, preventing illegal immigrants from entering the country, or fighting terrorists.

▼ Marine police help to keep our waterways safe by tackling drug smugglers, illegal immigrants, and other criminals.

The water police usually have a specialist underwater search and rescue unit. Police officers face diving up to 165 feet [50 meters] in murky waters looking for evidence, submerged vehicles, and even missing people in the most challenging of places. The officers working for these units face many dangers and undergo an intense diving course to carry out their job safely. Underwater officers are equipped with breathing apparatus, protective clothing, and special lighting. **Sonar technology** helps divers detect objects by bouncing sound waves through the water, which then send a digital image back to the computer at the surface.

▼ An underwater unit searches a swollen river for evidence following a crime.

"Hypodermic needles, builders' rubble, traffic cones—everything you can imagine is down there. Because you can't see, you're doing fingertip searches, and you learn to recognize everything by touch."

Sgt Stewart Kennedy, London's Metropolitan Police's Marine Policing Unit, UK

RIOTS

Sometimes police officers are faced with shocking violence when rioting hits the streets. Most police officers are trained in public order to control, disperse, and arrest unruly civilians to prevent destruction and violence in these situations.

When police officers are called in to oversee peaceful protests or control crowds their safety comes first.

As well as their standard equipment a police officer attending a protest or riot wears special, protective equipment:
Riot helmet with face visor   Body armor
Neck protection   Gas mask   Kneepads   Riot shield

Rodney King riots, 1992
Fierce rioting broke out in Los Angeles in April 1992, when a jury cleared four white police officers for assault of black motorist Rodney King. Riots erupted in the city's black neighborhoods with lootings and attacks on whites and Asians. The riots resulted in 55 deaths and over 2,000 people were injured, with police officers making over 12,000 arrests.

▼ Police officers wear full safety riot equipment when policing riots and protests.

"I think any police force in the world would have found it extremely difficult to cope with the rapidly escalating violence that we experienced in London. More than 250 officers were injured during the riots and many of them are still suffering as a result of these injuries."

Paul McKeever, chairman of the Police Federation of England and Wales, following the August 2011 riots

DANGER HOTSPOTS

Mexico

In Mexico, several drug cartels are fighting for the control of drug trafficking routes into the United States. The Mexican government has 50,000 troops and federal police involved in the fight against these cartels, but the number of deaths are increasing and are extremely violent. Mass graves, beheadings, and hangings from bridges are just some of the ugly sights that officers have witnessed in this war.

> **"** This is indeed a crisis. The rate at which our officers are being callously gunned down is extremely alarming... I have attended funerals of my police officers every weekend in the past four weeks. **"**
>
> **Mexican President Felipe Calderón**

Afghanistan

The Afghanistan police force are taking over security of the country with the withdrawal of **NATO forces** and foreign combat troops. These police officers face many dangers. Some of the dangers include roadside bombs, kidnapping, and vicious attacks at police checkpoints.

South Africa

Being a police officer in a country where 50 murders, 400 burglaries and over 500 violent assaults a day are reported is a very dangerous job. Where 4.2 million people are surviving on less than one dollar a day, poverty is one of the major factors leading to violence. Officers that police this country risk death on a daily basis.

HI-JACKING HOT SPOT

▲ Afghanistan police officers tackle rioters in Kabul.

IT'S A FACT!

Every police dog costs around US$15,000 to buy, train, and look after. Police forces use money that has been seized from suspects engaged in drug trafficking to pay for the dogs.

In 1971 WPCs Margaret Goodacre and Ann McPherson made history by being the first women police officers to join the Metropolitan Police's Mounted (horse) Branch in London, UK.

The Drug Enforcement Administration (DEA) was set up in 1973 to deal with the effects of drugs on the rising crime rate.

The fastest speed ticketed by police was issued in Texas in 2003. The driver was arrested for driving at 242 mph (389 km/h) in a 75 mph (120 km/h) zone.

The United States Mint Police are used 24 hours a day to protect over $100 billion in gold, silver, and other assets that are stored all over the U.S.

In March 2011, the United States had over 800,000 police officers available for duty and the United Kingdom had 137,000.

Police officers online
www.usacops.com
www.rcmp-grc.gc.ca
www.torontopolice.on.ca

GLOSSARY

air support unit A police unit that uses a helicopter to observe and help police officers on the ground.

cardiopulmonary resuscitation (CPR) An emergency procedure which is performed to restore the flow of blood to the brain and heart.

CCTV (closed-circuit television) Video cameras used for security and surveillance purposes.

drug cartel A criminal gang that operates and profits from illegal drugs.

E-FIT (Electronic Facial Identification Technique) Technology used to produce a computer-generated image of a suspect.

infiltrate To enter or gain membership to a group of people, slowly and secretively.

mounted unit Police officers that patrol on horses.

NATO forces An alliance of international military forces.

people trafficking Illegally transporting people through borders into new countries for profit.

personal protection pouch (PPP) A pouch carried by officers that contains gloves and a CPR mask.

police negotiator A specially trained police officer who talks with offenders in hostile situations.

sonar technology Underwater technology that can produce an image from bouncing sound waves through water.

suppressed weapons Weapons that do not produce noise when fired.

S.W.A.T. (special weapons and tactics team) A specially trained team of police officers who attend to very dangerous situations.

Taser A weapon used by police officers that gives out an electric shock when fired.

INDEX